LEGO® WOMEN OF NASA

Space Heroes

by Hannah Dolan

DK | Penguin Random House

Editor Joseph Stewart
Designers Sam Bartlett and James McKeag
Pre-production Producer Marc Staples
Producer Louise Daly
Managing Editor Paula Regan
Managing Art Editor Jo Connor
Publisher Julie Ferris
Art Director Lisa Lanzarini
Publishing Director Simon Beecroft

Reading Consultant Linda B. Gambrell, Ph.D

LEGO Ideas set designed by Maia Weinstock.

Dorling Kindersley would like to thank Randi Sørensen,
Paul Hansford and Martin Leighton Lindhardt at the LEGO Group.

First American Edition, 2018
Published in the United States by DK Publishing
345 Hudson Street, New York, New York 10014

18 19 20 21 10 9 8 7 6 5 4 3 2 1
001–309517–Feb/2018

Page design copyright ©2018 Dorling Kindersley Limited
DK, a Division of Penguin Random House LLC

DK books are available at special discounts when
purchased in bulk for sales promotions, premiums,
fund-raising, or educational use. For details, contact:
DK Publishing Special Markets,
345 Hudson Street, New York, New York 10014
SpecialSales@dk.com

ISBN 978-1-4654-7291-5 (Hardcover)
ISBN 978-1-4654-7290-8 (Paperback)

Printed and bound in U.S.A.

www.dk.com
www.LEGO.com

A WORLD OF IDEAS:
SEE ALL THERE IS TO KNOW

Contents

4   Out of this world
6   The women of NASA
8   Looking at space
10 Clever computers
12 Science star
14 Amazing astronaut
16 Space travel
18 Blastoff!
20 Space stars
22 Quiz
23 Index

Out of this world

People who work at NASA are interested in space.

They study space to learn more about it.
They also find ways to explore space.

The women of NASA

Let's meet four women who did great things at NASA.

Margaret Hamilton is a computer scientist.

Nancy Grace Roman is an astronomer.

Mae Jemison is
an astronaut.

Sally Ride was
an astronaut, too.

Looking at space

Nancy Grace Roman studies stars and planets.
She is called an astronomer.

Telescope
picture —

Nancy helped to create the
Hubble Space Telescope.
Hubble orbits Earth.
It sends back pictures of
faraway stars and planets.

Clever computers

Margaret Hamilton is a computer scientist.

Books of code

Margaret wrote a computer code for a spacecraft. The code told the spacecraft how to get to the moon!

Science star

Sally Ride was the first American woman to visit space. Sally also liked teaching children about science. Maybe one day they will become scientists, too!

Amazing astronaut

Mae Jemison trained as a doctor.

She became a NASA astronaut, too.

She was the first African-American woman in space.

Space travel

Endeavour is a space shuttle. It can carry seven NASA astronauts into space.

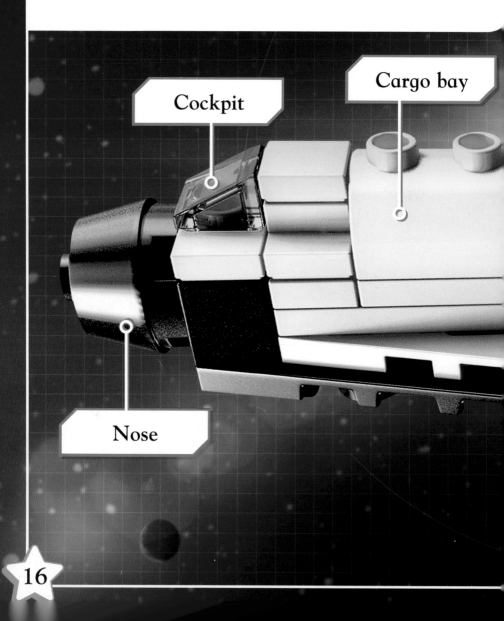

Cockpit

Cargo bay

Nose

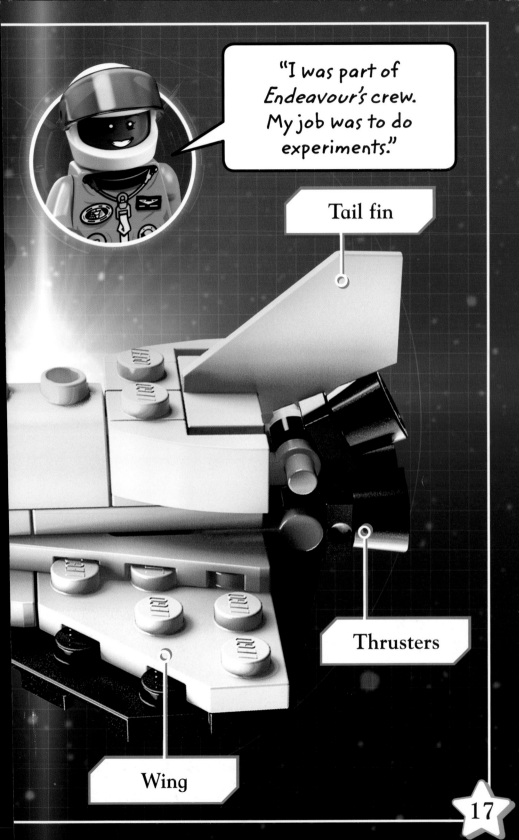

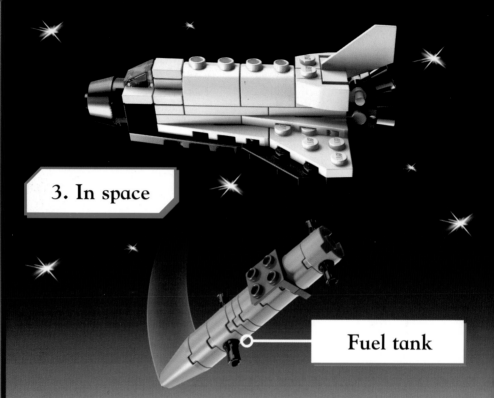

3. In space

Fuel tank

Blastoff!

Space shuttles need powerful boosters to get to space. First the shuttle takes off. Then the boosters detach. Finally, the fuel tank detaches. The shuttle is now in space!

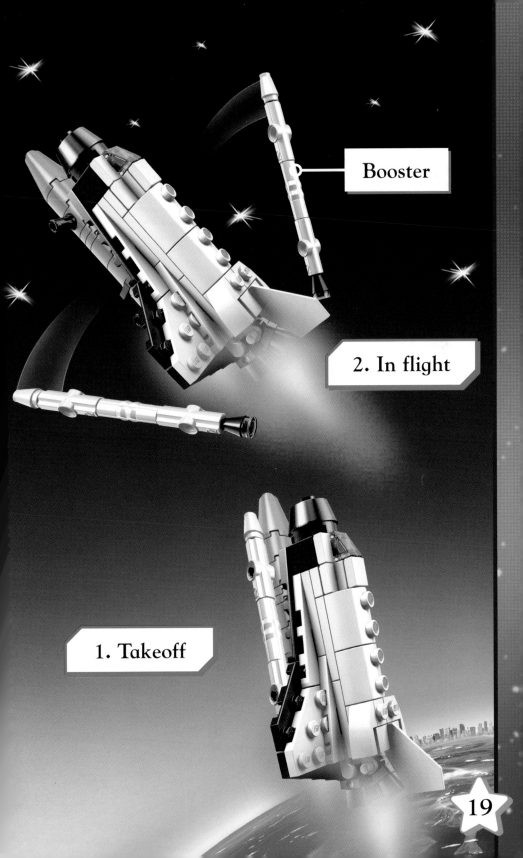

Booster

2. In flight

1. Takeoff

19

Space stars

These women of NASA have helped us get to the moon. They have also helped us to learn about space. They have changed our world. One day, you could too!

Quiz

1. What does an astronomer study?

2. What woman astronomer helped create the Hubble Space Telescope?

3. Who was the first American woman in space?

4. How many astronauts can Space Shuttle *Endeavour* carry?

5. What did Margaret Hamilton write to help a spacecraft fly to the moon?

Index

computer code 11

Space Shuttle
  Endeavour 14, 16–17

Hubble Telescope 9

Mae Jemison 7,
  14–15, 17, 20

Margaret Hamilton 6,
  10-11, 20

Nancy Grace Roman
  6, 8-9, 20

NASA 4, 6, 14, 16, 21

Sally Ride 7, 12-13, 20

Answers to the quiz on page 22

1. Stars and planets 2. Nancy Grace Roman 3. Sally Ride 4. Seven
5. A computer code

A LEVEL FOR EVERY READER

This book is a part of an exciting four-level reading series to support children in developing the habit of reading widely for both pleasure and information. Each book is designed to develop a child's reading skills, fluency, grammar awareness, and comprehension in order to build confidence and enjoyment when reading.

Ready for a Level 1 (Learning to Read) book
A child should:
- be familiar with most letters and sounds.
- understand how to blend sounds together to make words.
- have an awareness of syllables and rhyming sounds.

A valuable and shared reading experience
For many children, learning to read requires much effort, but adult participation can make reading both fun and easier. Here are a few tips on how to use this book with an early reader:

Check out the contents together:
- tell the child the book title and talk about what the book might be about.
- read about the book on the back cover and talk about the contents page to help heighten interest and expectation.
- chat about the pictures on each page.
- discuss new or difficult words.

Support the reader:
- give the book to the young reader to turn the pages.
- if the book seems too hard, support the child by sharing the reading task.

Talk at the end of each page:
- ask questions about the text and the meaning of the words used—this helps develop comprehension skills.
- read the quiz at the end of the book and encourage the reader to answer the questions, if necessary, by turning back to the relevant pages to find the answers.

Series consultant, Dr. Linda Gambrell, Distinguished Professor of Education at Clemson University, has served as President of the National Reading Conference, the College Reading Association, and the International Reading Association.